About the Author

Mrs. Jyoti Giramkar has 10 years of experience in Selenium Webdriver. She has developed automation frameworks using Selenium Webdriver in Java.

Her hobbies are travelling to new tourist places, watching football, cricket and learning latest technological stuff.

A special note of Thanks to My Husband

I would like to dedicate this book to my lovely husband for loving me so much and helping me write this book. Without his support, this book would not have been a reality.

Preface

This book is for automation tester who want to design the framework in selenium webdriver in Java. This book contains complete source codes and examples in Selenium Webdriver in Java.

Major topics covered in this book are.
1. Automation frameworks in Selenium
2. Data driven automation frameworks(DDF)
3. Keyword driven automation frameworks(KDF)
4. Hybrid driven automation frameworks(HDF)

1. Test Automation frameworks

In this chapter, you will learn about the test automation and why we should use the framework and what are the types of automation frameoworks out there to choose from.

1.1 Test Automation - Introduction

Test automation is the process of automating the manual testing activities. When the software is ready for test, we can verify and validate it either manually or by automation. If the software is huge with lot of modules in it, We need many testers to test it. Whenever there is a change in the software, We will have to again test it to verify that it meets the requirements and there is no defect in it.

Manually Testing the application has below disadvantages.
1. Time consuming
2. Costly
3. Cumbersome
4. Quality not assured due to human mistakes
5. Time constraints
6. Repeatative and hence Boring

By automating the testing process, we can overcome above challenges in testing process. You can use any tool like QTP , Selenium or Test Complete etc. In this book, we are going to use Selenium Webdriver tool.

1.2 Test Automation Frameworks - Introduction

Well – now that you know why automation is required in software testing, it is a time to understand the best practises used in test automation industry. As of 2014, QTP is the most popular automation testing tool in the market followed by TestComplete and Selenium Webdriver. The striking difference between selenium and QTP is that Selenium is open source tool which only supports Web application testing.

While QTP is a licensed tool offered by HP and it supports wide variety of desktop applications built in .Net, Java along with Web applications.

But Now a days Selenium Webdriver is gaining lot of popularity over QTP as far as testing of web applications is concerned.So it will be very helpful to know about the frameworks that can be used in Selenium Webdriver.

Now let us define the term – **Automation Framework**. The automation framework is nothing but the set of guidelines and conventions to follow when designing the code to test the software. When we follow these guidelines while developing the automation code, it helps to make automation testing more beneficial and scalable.

A test automation framework is an integrated system that sets the rules of automation of a specific product. This system integrates the function libraries, test data sources, object details and various reusable modules. These components act as small building blocks which needs to be assembled to represent a business process. The framework provides the basis of test automation and simplifies the automation effort.

1.3 Why Test Automation framework?

Since many tools provide record and playback feature, People usually rely on it. But this is not a good practise. When the

project is very big consisting of lot of modules, it is very important to have a automation framework in place.
The automation framework provides below advantages.

1. Proper oraganisation of test data.
2. Automation of new test cases is fast and simple.
3. Custom HTML or Excel reports along with Charts.
4. High Code Reusability.
5. Easy to maintain and enhance.
6. Easy to learn.

1.4 Types of Automation framework

There are many kinds of automation frameworks based upon the testing phase like Unit testing and System testing. Here is the list of **Unit testing frameworks**.

1. Junit (Java)
2. TestNG (Java)
3. Nunit (C#.Net)
4. unittest (Python)
5. Test::Unit (Ruby)

Here is the list of **System testing frameworks.**

1. Data Driven Framework
2. Keyword Driven Framework
3. Hybrid Framework (Data + Keyword)

Unit testing frameworks are used by developers to test the software. As a system tester, our job is to test the system as a black box. So here on we will be discussing only about system testing automation frameworks.

1.5 Which framework to choose?

We have to consider below factors when selecting the framework.

1. Size of the application
2. Time Constraints
3. Budget Constraints

2. Data driven Automation framework

In this chapter, you will learn about how to design data driven automation frameworks in Selenium Webdriver.

2.1 Data driven automation framework

In data driven frameworks, we store the test data seperately in the excel sheet and then we repeat the testing of each test data candidate with same code.

Below example will demonstrate how we can use data driven framework in Selenium.

Suppose we have a web application where in User will have to choose the User Id while doing the registration. The user Id should comply with below rules.

1. It should be at least 8 characters in length.
2. It should contain at least one Upper case alphabet character.
3. It should contain at least one digit.
4. It should not contain # character.

To test this feature, we can create the test data as shown in below figure and then write the code in Selenium Webdriver to pick up one User Id at a time and try to do the registration.

	A	B	C	D	E
1	TestID	UserID	Expected Result	Actual Result	Test Status
2	1	test1	Reject		
3	2	test17889	Reject		
4	3	tesT9080	Accept		
5	4	tesT#080	Reject		

Figure 1 - Sample Test Data Sheet

As shown in previous figure, we have created the test data sheet containing different User IDs we want to test. We have also mentioned which User Ids should be accepeted by the System and which ones should be rejected.

The excel sheet after the execution is shown below.

	A	B	C	D	E
1	TestID	UserID	Expected Result	Actual Result	Test Status
2	1	test1	Reject	Rejected	Pass
3	2	test17889	Reject	Rejected	Pass
4	3	tesT9080	Accept	Accepted	Pass
5	4	tesT#080	Reject	Accepted	Fail

Figure 2 - Sample Test Data after execution

From selenium script, we can read each row in the excel sheet and test the user Id one by one. Based upon the actual result, we can mark the test status as Pass or Fail as shown in previous figure.

We are going to see how to read excel sheet data from selenium in next chapters.

2.2 When to use Data driven automation framework

We can use data driven frameworks when

1. The features to test are very less.

2. We have to automate the test cases very fast.
3. Application size is very small.
4. We have to test the same functionality with lot of combinations of the test data.

3. Keyword driven Automation framework

In this chapter, you will learn about how to design keyword driven automation frameworks in Selenium Webdriver.

The Keyword driven framework has 4 main components.

1. Selenium Webdriver
2. Main driver method
3. Reporting (HTML Reports)
4. Function Library (Test/Keyword Library)
5. Test Data (Test Cases)

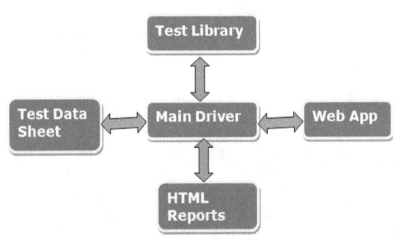

Figure 3 - Keyword driven framework Components

Let's have a look at each of these components.

3.1 Test Data

We validate the requirements of the software by executing test cases. Each test case has specific number of steps. We can convert these manual steps into automation by writing the methods to perform specific operations.

Sample Test data sheet is shown in below figure. The important columns in this excel sheet are mentioned below.

1. ID – Unique test case Id
2. Test Case Name – Test Case Name
3. Execution Flag – to Execute or not to execute test case
4. Test Step Id – Step id of the test case
5. Test Case Steps – Step name
6. Business Keyword – Business Keyword (Mapped to method)
7. Object Types – Class Types of the controls like webedit, weblist, webbutton
8. Object Names – Names of the controls linktext:Next;linktext:Previous;linktext:Back
9. Object Values – Values to enter /operation to perform on control
10. Parameter1 – parameter to control the method flow
11. Parameter2 – parameter to control the method flow
12. Parameter3 – parameter to control the method flow

	A	B	C	D	E	F
			Exec_ Flag	Test_step _ID		
1	ID	test_case_name	Flag	_ID	Test_case_steps	keyword
2	1	Test Name	Y	step1	xls_Enter_Data	xls_Enter_Data
3				step2	xls_Verify_Data	xls_Verify_Data
4	2	Test Name	Y	step1	xls_Enter_Data	xls_Enter_Data
5				step2	xls_Verify_Data	xls_Verify_Data

Figure 4 – Test Data Sheet (Columns A-F)

	G	H	I	J	K
	objectTypes	objectnames	objectvalues	parameter1	parameter2
	webedit;webedit	name:name;name:login	sagar;reply2sagar		
	webedit;webedit	name:name;name:login	sagar;reply2sagar		
	webedit;webedit	name:name;name:login	sagar;reply2sagar		
	webedit;webedit	name:name;name:login	sagar;reply2sagard		

Figure 5 - Test Data Sheet (Columns G-K)

Each manual test case is converted to automation test case as shown in above figure. Each automated step corresponds to the method.

If any of the test step of the test case fails, whole test case will fail. So to mark the test case as pass, you should have all the steps of the test cases passed. Main method will read each row in the data sheet one by one and call the corresponding method (keyword) which will perform specific operation on the given elements on the webpage.

3.2 Selenium Webdriver

If you know selenium installation in Eclipse, you can skip this section.

Installing Selenium in Eclipse.
Those who are new to the Selenium Webdriver and Eclipse, let me explain how to install selenium in Eclipse.

Well – Now let us understand the installation steps in selenium.

The list of Softwares you will need is given below.

1. Java JDK

2. Eclipse – Popular Java IDE

3. Selenium Java API (jar file)

    @https://code.google.com/p/selenium/downloads/list

4. Web driver for Chrome (exe file)

    @https://code.google.com/p/selenium/downloads/list

You can easily check if Java JDK is installed in windows system using command ">java –version" in command prompt.

```
C:\Users\sagar>java -version
java version "1.6.0"
Java(TM) SE Runtime Environment (build 1.6.0-b105)
Java HotSpot(TM) Client VM (build 1.6.0-b105, mixed mode, sharing)
```

Figure 6 - Java Command

If you get the output as shown in figure, that means you have already java installed in your system. But if you get error saying Java is not recognized as internal or external command, Then you will have to install jdk in your system.

To install jdk you can visit below url

http://www.oracle.com/technetwork/java/javase/downloads

To install eclipse you can visit below url

https://www.eclipse.org/downloads

You can download Most of the selenium related files at

http://docs.seleniumhq.org/download/

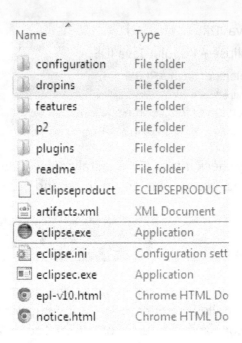

Name	Type
configuration	File folder
dropins	File folder
features	File folder
p2	File folder
plugins	File folder
readme	File folder
.eclipseproduct	ECLIPSEPRODUCT
artifacts.xml	XML Document
eclipse.exe	Application
eclipse.ini	Configuration sett
eclipsec.exe	Application
epl-v10.html	Chrome HTML Do
notice.html	Chrome HTML Do

Figure 7 - Eclipse Folder Structure

After you download eclipse in zip format, you will have to unzip it. Folder structure of the eclipse after unzipping is shown in previuos figure.

To launch eclipse, you will have double click on the eclipse.exe file.

Once you have these softwares with you, You can follow below steps.

- Open Eclipse and create new Java Project.
- Create a package and class with name SampleTest in it.
- Go to project properties and select Java build path. Select libraries tab and then choose add external jar.
- Browse to the jar file you have downloaded in step 3 in first list above.
- Select apply and close

Below images will give you the idea of how to create a project in Eclipse.

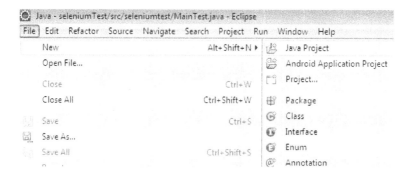

Figure 8 - Add New Java Project in Eclipse

In File menu, you have to click on new and then click on the Java Project. In new Java project window you will have to enter the name of the project and select the JRE.

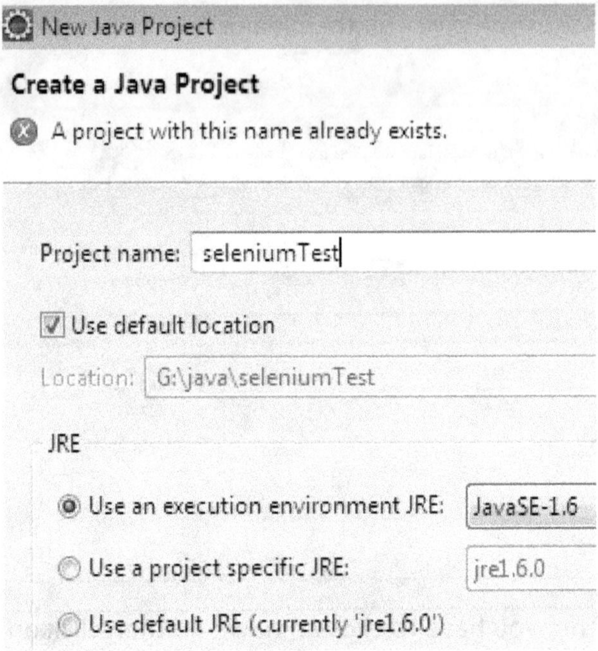

Figure 9 - Add new Project in Eclipse

To work with selenium webdriver, you will have to add external selenium Jar library reference by going to project properties window -> Java build path -> libraries and then click on Add external Jar. As shown in next figure, I have added selenium-server-standalone-2.35.jar library file to project.
By adding a selenium jar library file, you will be able to access the selenium classes defined in the org.openqa.selenium package and it's subpackages.

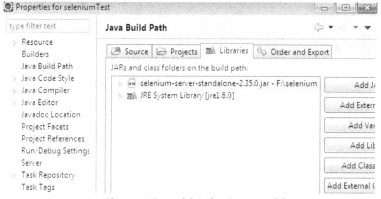

Figure 10 - Add Selenium Jar library

Next step is to create a package in the project that we have created. To add a package, right click on the folder called src under project and then select new. You will find options as shown in next image. Select package.

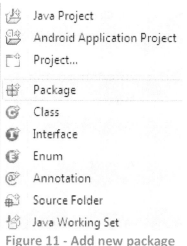

Figure 11 - Add new package

After you click on the package, you will see new package window. You will have to enter the name of package. As a convention, package names should be in small cap letters.

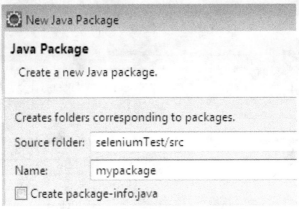

Figure 42 - Provide the name of package

Now you can add Java class, by right clicking on the package you have just added.

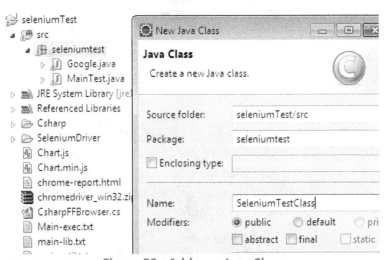

Figure 53 - Add new Java Class

In new Java class window, you will have to enter the name of class. As a convention, first letter of class name should be in upper case. When you click on finish, sample class code will be automatically created for you as shown in next image.

```
J *SeleniumTestClass.java ⋈
    package seleniumtest;

    public class SeleniumTestClass {

        /**
         * @param args
         */
        public static void main(String[] args) {
            // TODO Auto-generated method stub



        }

    }
```

Figure 64 - Sample Java Class Code

Now it is time to write some code in the main method and run the java program.

I have added just one line of code in the main method as shown in next figure.

```
System.out.println("First Java program in Eclipse");
```

Above line will print the string passed in as a parameter. To run the code, you will have to click on the run button (green ball button containing white arrow). To debug the code, you will have to click on the button looking like bug.

Run SeleniumTestClass

SeleniumTestClass.java

```
package seleniumtest;

public class SeleniumTestClass {

    /**
     * @param args
     */
    public static void main(String[] args) {
        // TODO Auto-generated method stub
System.out.println("First Java program in Eclipse");
    }

}
```

Problems @ Javadoc Declaration Console Lint War

<terminated> SeleniumTestClass [Java Application] C:\Program Files\Java\
First Java program in Eclipse

Figure 15 - Running a Java Code

After you run the program, you can see the ouput in the console window.

Selenium webdriver is a driver instance for each browser. In selenium 2.0, there is a separate implementation for each browser. For example – If you want to automate the chrome browser, you will have to create the instance of the chrome driver as shown in below statement.

```
//launching the chrome browser
//Please import classes from package
org.openqa.selenium.chrome
```

```
//give the path of the webdriver exe

System.setProperty("webdriver.chrome.driver",
"C:\\chromedriver.exe");

//create the instance of the chromedriver.

WebDriver wb =  new ChromeDriver();
```

Similarly we can create the driver instance for other browsers
like FireFox, Internet Explorer, Safari , Andriod , iPhone etc.

```
//launching the Internet explorer browser
//Please import classes from package
org.openqa.selenium.ie

System.setProperty("webdriver.ie.driver",
"C:\\chromedriver.exe");
WebDriver wb =  new InternetExplorerDriver();
```

```
//launching the FireFox browser
//Please import classes from package
org.openqa.selenium.firefox
WebDriver wb =  new FirefoxDriver();
```

```
//launching the Safari browser
//Please import classes from package
org.openqa.selenium.safari
WebDriver wb =  new SafariDriver();
```

3.3 Main driver method

For our framework, we are going to create 4 Java Source Files.

1. **TestDriver.Java** (Contains main driver method).
2. **Keyword_Library.Java** (Contains methods to perform specific operation on application).
3. **Helpers.Java** (Contains methods to create reports and also provides global variables).

This is the main method in Java class (**TestDriver.Java**) that will drive the execution of functional test cases. We are going to store the test cases in the Excel sheet. Main method will read all test cases one by one and then execute them.
Main method is the heart of our Keyword driven automation framework. It will co-ordinate with all other components as decribed below.

1. Read the Keyword and related test parameters of test cases from Test Data sheet.
2. Each keyword in the test case is mapped to the method in our framework.
3. Main method will call the functionality specific method in the keyword library corresponding to the keyword in the test case.
4. All the actions that selenium webdriver is performing are logged in the html file using reporting module as and when particular keyword is executing.
5. When the method (Keyword) is executed, it returns the true or false boolean value based upon the execution status of the method. If the method is executed successfully, it returns true otherwise It returns false flag.

6. Main method also keeps the pass and fail counters to record how many test cases have passed and how many have failed.

Please note that we have to import classes from Apache POI library to work with Excel files.

```
import org.apache.poi.hssf.usermodel.HSSFSheet;
import
org.apache.poi.hssf.usermodel.HSSFWorkbook;
import org.apache.poi.ss.usermodel.Row;
```

Here is the complete source code of the **TestDriver.Java** file.

```
import java.awt.Desktop;
import java.io.File;
import java.io.FileInputStream;
import java.io.FileNotFoundException;
import java.io.IOException;
import java.lang.reflect.Method;
import java.text.DecimalFormat;
import java.util.ArrayList;
import java.util.Iterator;
import java.util.List;
import java.util.concurrent.TimeUnit;

import org.apache.poi.hssf.usermodel.HSSFSheet;
import
org.apache.poi.hssf.usermodel.HSSFWorkbook;
import org.apache.poi.ss.usermodel.Row;
import org.openqa.selenium.By;

import org.openqa.selenium.WebDriver;
```

```java
import org.openqa.selenium.chrome.ChromeDriver;
import org.openqa.selenium.interactions.*;
import org.openqa.selenium.Keys;

import
org.openqa.selenium.ElementNotVisibleException;

@SuppressWarnings("unused")
class TestDriver
{


public  static int totalPass,totalFail = 0;
     public  static int execCounter = 0;
     public static WebDriver driver;


     public static void main(String [] arg)

     {

java.util.Date currentDate = new
java.util.Date();
long t1 = currentDate.getTime();

//File profileDir = new
File("C:\\Users\\jyoti.giramkar\\AppData\\Roamin
g\\Mozilla\\Firefox\\Profiles\\qjpuns9y.default"
);
//FirefoxProfile profile = new
FirefoxProfile(profileDir);
//driver =  new FirefoxDriver(profile);

//System.setProperty("webdriver.ie.driver",
"F:\\selenium\\IEDriverServer.exe");
//driver =  new InternetExplorerDriver();
```

```java
System.setProperty("webdriver.chrome.driver",
"F:\\chromedriver.exe");
driver =  new ChromeDriver();

//driver = new SafariDriver();

driver.get(Environment.url);
String browser = "";

if (driver.toString().contains("chrome"))
{
     browser = "chrome";

}
else if (driver.toString().contains("fire"))
{
     browser = "firefox";

}
else if (driver.toString().contains("explorer"))
{
     browser = "IE";

}

//for each browser, there will be separate
report file

Helpers.ResultFile = Helpers.ResultFile + "\\" +
browser + "-report.html";

driver.manage().timeouts().implicitlyWait(20,
TimeUnit.SECONDS);
```

```java
driver.manage().timeouts().pageLoadTimeout(50,Ti
meUnit.SECONDS);

driver.manage().window().maximize();

FileInputStream file = null;
HSSFWorkbook workbook;

//Helpers class has a method to create header
section of the html report..

Helpers.createHtmlHead(1);


try {

//open the test data sheet file.
//batch_selenium.xls

    file = new FileInputStream(new
File("F:\\selenium\\batch_selenium.xls"));

//Get the workbook instance for XLS file
    workbook = new HSSFWorkbook(file);

  //Get first sheet from the workbook
HSSFSheet sheet = workbook.getSheetAt(0);

//Iterate through each row from first sheet
  Iterator<Row> rowIterator = sheet.iterator();
  int k=0;
 while (rowIterator.hasNext())
            {
            rowIterator.next();
            k++;
            }
```

```java
//   sheet.getRow(0);
 int intRowCounter=1;
   while(intRowCounter<k) {

        Row row =  sheet.getRow(intRowCounter);


//Helpers class has another method to read data
from excel sheet cell.

   ExcelParams.Exec_Flag =
Helpers.readcell(row,2);

   String strExecutionflag =
ExcelParams.Exec_Flag;


if    (strExecutionflag.equalsIgnoreCase("Y") )
{

      execCounter++;
      //clear temp log
Helpers.gtestcaselog.setLength(0);

driver.getTitle();

java.util.Date currentDate2 = new
java.util.Date();
long testcasestart = currentDate2.getTime();



            boolean blnTestStepFlag = true;
            boolean    blnOverallTestCaseStatus =
true;
```

```java
            String strTestCaseID =
ExcelParams.Test_Step_ID =
Helpers.readcell(row,3);
            String strTest_Case_Name =
ExcelParams.Test_Case_Name =
Helpers.readcell(row,1);
            String gtestcaselog = "" ;
ExcelParams.ID = Helpers.readcell(row,0);

//Reinitialize the log for new test case


while(blnTestStepFlag)
{



    ExcelParams.Test_Case_Steps =
Helpers.readcell(row,4);
    ExcelParams.Business_Keyword =
Helpers.readcell(row,5);
    ExcelParams.objectTypes =
Helpers.readcell(row,6);
    ExcelParams.objectNames =
Helpers.readcell(row,7);
    ExcelParams.objectValues =
Helpers.readcell(row,8);
    ExcelParams.parameter1 =
Helpers.readcell(row,9);
    ExcelParams.parameter2 =
Helpers.readcell(row,11);
    ExcelParams.parameter3 =
Helpers.readcell(row,12);
```

```java
try{

TestDriver.driver.manage().timeouts().implicitly
Wait(20, TimeUnit.SECONDS);
        Helpers.createTestCaseLog(" Calling
method " + (ExcelParams.Business_Keyword), 5);

        Method method =
FunctionLibrary.class.getMethod((ExcelParams.Bus
iness_Keyword).trim());
        boolean ret = (Boolean)
method.invoke(null);



        if (ret == false)
            blnOverallTestCaseStatus =
false;


}


catch(Exception e){

        //Futil.createTestCaseLog("Test
Failed" , 2);
System.out.println(e.toString());
blnOverallTestCaseStatus = false;
Helpers.createTestCaseLog("Exception Message " +
e.getMessage() + e.toString(), 2);
    }


    intRowCounter++;
```

```
    row = sheet.getRow(intRowCounter);


    if (blnOverallTestCaseStatus == false ||
(Helpers.readcell(row,5)).equalsIgnoreCase("")
||
("Step1".equalsIgnoreCase((Helpers.readcell(row,
3)).trim())))
    {
        intRowCounter--;
        break;
    }


}//Loop until blnTestStepFlag = true

//log the result for each test case



if (blnOverallTestCaseStatus==true)
{
        totalPass++;
}
else
{
        totalFail++;
}

//strTestCaseID,byval strTest_Case_Name,byval
blnOverallTestCaseStatus
java.util.Date currentDate1 = new
java.util.Date();
long testcaseended = currentDate1.getTime();
```

```java
String executionTime =
Helpers.getTimeDiff(testcasestart,
testcaseended,"min");

Helpers.createTestReport(
execCounter,ExcelParams.ID,
ExcelParams.Test_Case_Name,blnOverallTestCaseSta
tus,executionTime );


}     //if exec_flag = true

intRowCounter++;
}     //loop until usedRange

  java.util.Date currentDate2 = new
java.util.Date();
     long t2 = currentDate2.getTime();
     String TotalexecutionTime =
Helpers.getTimeDiff(t1, t2,"min");

System.out.println("Test Execution Time in
Minutes...." + TotalexecutionTime);
System.out.println("Pass Test Cases...." +
totalPass);
System.out.println("Fail test cases...." +
totalFail);

Helpers.appendToFile(Helpers.ResultFile,
"</tbody></table>");


String strSummaryHTML ="";
```

```
strSummaryHTML = strSummaryHTML + "<script
type='text/javascript'
src='http://www.google.com/jsapi'></script>";
strSummaryHTML = strSummaryHTML + "<script
type='text/javascript'>";
strSummaryHTML = strSummaryHTML +
"google.load('visualization', '1', {packages:
['corechart']});";
strSummaryHTML = strSummaryHTML + "</script>";
strSummaryHTML = strSummaryHTML + "<script
type='text/javascript'>";
strSummaryHTML = strSummaryHTML + "  function
drawVisualization() {";
    // Create and populate the data table.
strSummaryHTML = strSummaryHTML + "var data =
google.visualization.arrayToDataTable([";
strSummaryHTML = strSummaryHTML + " ['Task',
'Hours per Day'],";
strSummaryHTML = strSummaryHTML + "['pass', " +
totalPass +"],";
strSummaryHTML = strSummaryHTML + "['fail', " +
totalFail +"]";
strSummaryHTML = strSummaryHTML + "]);";


strSummaryHTML = strSummaryHTML + "var options =
{";
strSummaryHTML = strSummaryHTML +    "    title:
'Test Report',";
strSummaryHTML = strSummaryHTML + "
colors:['green','red'],";
strSummaryHTML = strSummaryHTML + "};";
```

```
strSummaryHTML = strSummaryHTML + "new
google.visualization.PieChart(document.getElemen
tById('visualization')).";
strSummaryHTML = strSummaryHTML + "  draw(data,
options);";
strSummaryHTML = strSummaryHTML + "}";


strSummaryHTML = strSummaryHTML + "
google.setOnLoadCallback(drawVisualization);";
strSummaryHTML = strSummaryHTML + "</script>";


String temp = "'<table
style=\\'width:300px\\'>";

temp = temp + "<tr><td>Pass : </td><td>" +
totalPass +  " </td> </tr><tr>";

DecimalFormat df=new DecimalFormat("0.00");
String avgTime =
df.format(Float.parseFloat(TotalexecutionTime)/(
totalPass+totalFail));

temp = temp + "<td>Failed : </td><td> " +
totalFail +  "</td> </tr></tr> <td>Total
Execution Time : </td><td>" + TotalexecutionTime
+  " min <br/> (Avg Time:" + avgTime + "
min)</td></tr></table>'" ;

strSummaryHTML = strSummaryHTML + "<script>
document.getElementById('passfail').innerHTML ="
+ temp;
strSummaryHTML = strSummaryHTML + "</script>";
```

```java
strSummaryHTML = strSummaryHTML +
"</body></html>" ;

Helpers.appendToFile(Helpers.ResultFile,
strSummaryHTML );




} catch (FileNotFoundException e) {
  e.printStackTrace();
} catch (IOException e) {
  e.printStackTrace();
}
finally{
    try{
        file.close();
        Thread.sleep(2000);
    }
    catch(Exception e){}

driver.close();
driver.quit();


            try{

            Desktop.getDesktop().open(new
File(Helpers.ResultFile));
            }catch(Exception e){}
    }
```

```
}//main method ends



}
```

Explaination –
1. In the first part of the program, we have imported required packages and classes.
2. Then we have declared below members of the Class.

```
public static WebDriver wb;
public static int
totalPass, totalFail = 0;
public   static int execCounter = 0;
```

3. Then we have a main method body. We have used Date class to record the time at which execution is started.

```
java.util.Date currentDate = new
java.util.Date();
long t1 = currentDate.getTime();
```

4. In the next statement, We have created the browser instance.

```
System.setProperty("webdriver.chrome.driver",
"C:\\chromedriver2.8.exe");
wb =  new ChromeDriver();
```

5. Next we have navigated to the url using below statement

```
wb.get(Environment.url);
```

6. Then we have set the path of the result file where we want to save the html reports

```
Futil.ResultFile = Futil.ResultFile +
"\\" + browser + "-report.html";
```

7. Next we have set the implicit timeouts for the driver using below syntax.

```
wb.manage().timeouts().implicitlyWait(20,
TimeUnit.SECONDS);
wb.manage().timeouts().pageLoadTimeout(50,Time
Unit.SECONDS);
```

8. Next statement will maximize the browser window. It is a good practise to maximize the window after you have launched the browser.

```
wb.manage().window().maximize();
```

9. Next statement will create html report header section. I will talk about the Futil Class later in this book. This class provides some of the methods to work with reports files and time/date management.

```
Futil.createHtmlHead(1);
```

10. Next we have created local variables to open the xls workbook file using below statements.

```
file = new FileInputStream(new
File("C:\\SelenuimProject\\book1.xls"));

//Get the workbook instance for XLS file
workbook = new HSSFWorkbook(file);

//Get first sheet from the workbook
HSSFSheet sheet = workbook.getSheetAt(1);
```

11. Now we have got the sheet reference in the variable sheet. To find total number of rows in the excel sheet we have used below code block.

```
//Iterate through each row from first sheet
```

```
Iterator<Row> rowIterator = sheet.iterator();
int k=0;
while (rowIterator.hasNext())
        {
                rowIterator.next();
                k++;
        }
```

12. In next line, our main code starts. In this loop we are iterating through each row in the excel sheet and trying to execute the keyword (mapped to method) in that row. We are reading the value in the Exec_Flag column. If the value in this column is equal to "Y" then we execute that test case else we just jump to next row.

```
while(intRowCounter<k) {

        //Iterate through each row from first
sheet (Test Data Sheet)
        Row row =  sheet.getRow(intRowCounter);


        //getNumericCellValue
        ExcelParams.Exec_Flag =
Futil.readcell(row,4);
        String strExecutionflag =
ExcelParams.Exec_Flag;

        if
        (strExecutionflag.equalsIgnoreCase("Y")
)


        {
        //Execute the test case
        }
```

```
..…..
..…..
//More lines of code

}
```

13. If the Exec_Flag is Y then we execute all steps in that test case.

```
execCounter++;    //test cases executed counter
Futil.gtestcaselog.setLength(0);
//reinitialize the log for each test case

boolean blnTestStepFlag = true;
boolean blnOverallTestCaseStatus = true;

//note down the test step id and test case
name

String strTestCaseID =
ExcelParams.Test_Step_ID =
Futil.readcell(row,5);
String strTest_Case_Name =
ExcelParams.Test_Case_Name =
Futil.readcell(row,3);

String gtestcaselog = "" ;
ExcelParams.ID = Futil.readcell(row,2);




while(blnTestStepFlag)
{

   //execute all steps in the test case until
blnTestStepFlag = true

}
```

14. Next we have to run the loop until either the testcase passes or fails. From each row we have to read the step details like business keyword, controlType, ControlName, ControlValues and parameters1/2/3. Then we are invoking the method mapped to the keyword using reflections. The return type of the method is either true or false. If the method returns true, that means test step passes else it fails.

```
        ExcelParams.Business_Keyword =
Futil.readcell(row,7);
        ExcelParams.ControlType =
Futil.readcell(row,8);
        ExcelParams.ControlName =
Futil.readcell(row,9);
        ExcelParams.ControlValues =
Futil.readcell(row,10);
        ExcelParams.parameter1 =
Futil.readcell(row,11);
        ExcelParams.parameter2 =
Futil.readcell(row,12);
        ExcelParams.parameter3 =
Futil.readcell(row,13);


   try{
        Futil.createTestCaseLog(" Calling method
" + (ExcelParams.Business_Keyword), 4);

        Method method =
FunctionLibrary.class.getMethod((ExcelParams.B
usiness_Keyword).trim());

        boolean ret = (boolean)
method.invoke(null);

        if (ret == false)
```

```
                    blnOverallTestCaseStatus = false;

    }
    catch(Exception e){

    blnOverallTestCaseStatus = false;
    Futil.createTestCaseLog("Exception Message "
+ e.getMessage() +    e.toString(), 2);
        }

        intRowCounter++;
        row = sheet.getRow(intRowCounter);

        if (blnOverallTestCaseStatus == false ||
(Futil.readcell(row,5)).equalsIgnoreCase("")
||
("Step1".equalsIgnoreCase((Futil.readcell(row,
5)).trim()))))
        {
           intRowCounter--;
           break;
        }
```

15. After the test fails or passes, we are incrementing the corresponding counters to keep track of how many test cases have passed and failed. We are also finding the total execution time required to execute the test case and writing the detailed log in the file at the end and then jumping to the next row in the excel sheet.

```
if (blnOverallTestCaseStatus==true)
{
        totalPass++;
}
else
{
        totalFail++;
```

```
}
java.util.Date currentDate1 = new
java.util.Date();
long testcaseended = currentDate1.getTime();
String executionTime =
Futil.getTimeDiff(testcasestart,
testcaseended,"min");
Futil.createTestReport(
execCounter,ExcelParams.ID,
ExcelParams.Test_Case_Name,blnOverallTestCaseS
tatus,executionTime );
```

16. Finally we are closing the reports using below statement. We are also writing the total pass and failed test cases to the report.

```
Futil.appendToFile(Futil.ResultFile,
"</tbody></table>");
```

17. At the end, We are closing the browser window and quiting the driver.

```
wb.close();
wb.quit();
```

3.4 Reporting

Now let us look at the reporting part of the framework. We are creating html reports for the automation execution. Please have a look at below reports.

Test Report

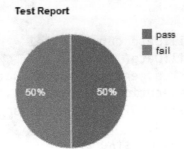

- pass
- fail

50% 50%

Pass :	1
Failed :	1
Total Execution Time :	0.54 min (Avg Time:0.27 min)

Report(Shrink/Expand)   Failed Only   Passed Only

No	Test_Id	Test_Case_Name
1	1	Test Name

Test_Description	Status
Calling method xls_Enter_Data Pass : Web Element webedit -> name:name found Info : Value entered is -> **sagar** Pass : Web Element webedit -> name:login found Info : Value entered is -> **reply2sagar** Calling method xls_Verify_Data Pass : Web Element webedit -> name:name found Pass : Actual value sagar and Expected sagar matching Pass : Web Element webedit -> name:login found Pass : Actual value reply2sagar and Expected reply2sagar matching	Pass..0.08m

Helpers.Java Source code is given below.

```java
import java.io.File;
import java.io.FileWriter;
import java.text.DecimalFormat;
import java.util.HashMap;
import java.util.Map;

import org.apache.poi.ss.usermodel.Row;



class Environment{

    public static String url =
"http://rediff.com";
public static String UID = "";
public static String Password = "";
public static String DataSheet = "";
public static String SheetName = "";
```

```java
//change the environment to production to
execute the test cases without showing
exceptions
public static String Env = "TEST";

	public static  Map<String, String> map =
new HashMap<String, String>();



	public static void value(String k, String
v)
	{

		map.put(k, v);

	}

	public static String getValue(String k)
	{

		return map.get(k);

	}

}


class ExcelParams{

}
```

```java
class Futil
{
    public static String
ResultFile="C:\\SelenuimProject\\reports";
public static StringBuffer gtestcaselog = new
StringBuffer("");



public static String readcell(Row rowObj,int
colNum)
{
    String x="";
try{
    if  (rowObj.getCell(colNum).getCellType()
== 1)
        x =
rowObj.getCell(colNum).getStringCellValue();
    else if
(rowObj.getCell(colNum).getCellType() == 0)
        x = "" +
(int)rowObj.getCell(colNum).getNumericCellValue(
);
}
catch(Exception e){
    x = "";
//System.out.println(e.toString() + " while
reading a cell");
    }

    return x;
}
```

```java
public static void killProcess(String Process){

    try{
    Runtime.getRuntime().exec("taskkill /IM "
+ Process);
    }catch(Exception ex){}
}




public static void writeCell(Row rowObj,int
colNum, String data)
{

    try{


rowObj.getCell(colNum).setCellValue((String)
data);

    }
    catch(Exception e){

        System.out.println(e.toString() + "
while writing a cell");
    }


}

public static String getTimeDiff(long t1, long
t2,String interval)
```

```java
{

        float diff = t2 - t1;

        if
(interval.equalsIgnoreCase("min"))
 diff = diff / (1000*60);
 else
 diff = diff / 1000;


 DecimalFormat df=new DecimalFormat("0.00");
 String formate = df.format(diff);
 //diff = (float)df.parse(formate) ;

            return   formate;


}

    public static void
createTestCaseLog(String str,int intStatus )
    {

        String strhtml="";
if (intStatus == 1)
strhtml = "<span style='color:green'> Pass :
</span> " ;
else if  (intStatus == 2)
strhtml = "<span style='color:red'> Fail  
: </span> ";
else if  (intStatus == 3)
strhtml = "<span style='color:maroon'> Warning :
</span> ";
```

```java
else if  (intStatus == 4)
strhtml = "<span> Info   : </span> " ;


gtestcaselog.append(strhtml).append(str).append(
"<br/>");



//testCaseLog = testCaseLog.append(s1);
}

public static void appendToFile(String
filePath,String data) {
     //This function will be used to append
text data to filepath
     try{
     File temp = new File(filePath);
     FileWriter fw = new FileWriter(temp,true);
     fw.append(data);
     fw.close();
     }catch(Exception e){}
}

public static void createHtmlHead(int param)
{
     param = 2;
     String strSummaryHTML= "";


strSummaryHTML = "<html><head><title>Report Of
Execution </title> ";

strSummaryHTML = strSummaryHTML + "<style> body
{ margin:auto; text-align:center; } table {
margin:auto; width:1200px; border:solid 2px
```

```
black; color:blue; font:normal 12px arial;
border-collapse:collapse;  } ";
strSummaryHTML = strSummaryHTML + "td { text-
align:center; border:solid 1px gray;
padding:7px; background-color:#F5F5DC }";
strSummaryHTML = strSummaryHTML +
"button,.desctd { cursor:pointer; }";
strSummaryHTML = strSummaryHTML + "th {
font:bold 16px arial; border:solid 1px gray;
padding:10px; background-color:#FFE4E1
}</style>";

strSummaryHTML = strSummaryHTML + "<script
src='http://ajax.googleapis.com/ajax/libs/jquery
/1.10.2/jquery.min.js'>";
strSummaryHTML = strSummaryHTML + "</script>";

strSummaryHTML = strSummaryHTML + "<script>";

strSummaryHTML = strSummaryHTML +
"$(document).ready(function(){";
strSummaryHTML = strSummaryHTML +
"$('.desc').slideToggle(1000);";
strSummaryHTML = strSummaryHTML + "
$('#se').click(function(){";
strSummaryHTML = strSummaryHTML + "
$('.desc').slideToggle(1000);";
strSummaryHTML = strSummaryHTML + " });";
strSummaryHTML = strSummaryHTML + " });";


strSummaryHTML = strSummaryHTML +
"$(document).ready(function(){";
strSummaryHTML = strSummaryHTML + "
$('#failonly').click(function(){";
```

```
strSummaryHTML = strSummaryHTML + "
$('.passtr').fadeOut(1000);";
strSummaryHTML = strSummaryHTML + "
$('.failtr').fadeIn(1000);";
strSummaryHTML = strSummaryHTML + " });";
strSummaryHTML = strSummaryHTML + " });";


strSummaryHTML = strSummaryHTML +
"$(document).ready(function(){";
strSummaryHTML = strSummaryHTML + "
$('#passonly').click(function(){";
strSummaryHTML = strSummaryHTML + "
$('.failtr').fadeOut(1000);";
strSummaryHTML = strSummaryHTML + "
$('.passtr').fadeIn(1000);";
strSummaryHTML = strSummaryHTML + " });";
strSummaryHTML = strSummaryHTML + " });";




strSummaryHTML = strSummaryHTML +
"$(document).ready(";
strSummaryHTML = strSummaryHTML + "function(){";
strSummaryHTML = strSummaryHTML +
"$('.desctd').click(";
strSummaryHTML = strSummaryHTML + "function(){";
strSummaryHTML = strSummaryHTML + "x =
this.previousSibling.firstChild;";
strSummaryHTML = strSummaryHTML +
"$(x).slideToggle(1000);";
strSummaryHTML = strSummaryHTML + "});";
strSummaryHTML = strSummaryHTML + "});";
```

```
strSummaryHTML = strSummaryHTML + "</script>";


strSummaryHTML = strSummaryHTML + "<script
src='Chart.js'></script>";
//strSummaryHTML = strSummaryHTML + "<script
src='query.js'></script>";


strSummaryHTML = strSummaryHTML + "<meta name =
'viewport' content = 'initial-scale = 1, user-
scalable = no'>";



strSummaryHTML = strSummaryHTML +  "</head>
<body>";



strSummaryHTML = strSummaryHTML +  "<table
id='top' style='table-
layout:fixed;width:1000px'> <tr> <td> <canvas
id='canvas' height='200' width='200'>Test
Report</canvas></td><td> <span style='font:16px
tahoma bold' id='passfail'></span> <br/> <button
id='se'>Report(Shrink/Expand)</button>
   <button id='failonly'> Failed Only
</button>    <button id='passonly'>
Passed Only </button>  </td></tr></table>";
```

```java
strSummaryHTML = strSummaryHTML + "<table
style='table-layout:fixed;width:1000px'>";
//strSummaryHTML = strSummaryHTML + "<tr><th
colspan=5> Detailed Report - <button>Toggle
Report(Shrink/Expand)</button> </th></tr>";
strSummaryHTML = strSummaryHTML +
"<thead><tr><th style='width:10%'>No</th><th
style='width:10%'>Test_Id</th><th
style='width:20%'>Test_Case_Name</th><th
style='width:50%'>Test_Description<br/></th><th>
Status</th></tr></thead></tbody>";

                 try{
                         if ((new
File(ResultFile)).exists() )
                                 (new
File(ResultFile)).delete();


        appendToFile(ResultFile,strSummaryHTML);
                 }catch(Exception e){}
}




public static void createTestReport(int
cnt,String TestId,String name,boolean b,String
time )
{
        String status="";
String toplink ="";
if (b==true)
        status = "<span
style='color:green'>Pass</span>";
else
```

```java
        status = "<span
style='color:red'>Fail</span>";

status = status + ".." + time + "m";
String strDetailedHTML = "";
if (cnt%10==0)
        toplink = "<br/><a href='#top'>Top</a>";
else
        toplink ="";

if (b==true)
strDetailedHTML = "<tr class='passtr'><td> " +
cnt + " </td><td>" + TestId + " </td><td> " +
name + " </td><td style='text-align:left;'><span
class='desc'> " + gtestcaselog +
"</span></td><td  class='desctd'> " + status +
toplink + "</td></tr>";
else
strDetailedHTML = "<tr class='failtr'><td> " +
cnt + " </td><td>" + TestId + " </td><td> " +
name + " </td><td style='text-align:left;'><span
class='desc'> " + gtestcaselog +
"</span></td><td class='desctd' >" + status +
toplink + "</td></tr>";

try{
        appendToFile(ResultFile,strDetailedHTML);
        }catch(Exception e){}

//testCaseLog = testCaseLog.append(s1);
        }

}
```

Important Classes in Futil.Java source file are.

1. Environment – used to store environment variables

```
try{
        File temp = new File(filePath);
        FileWriter fw = new FileWriter(temp,true);
        fw.append(data);
        fw.close();
        }
catch(Exception e){}
```

2. createHtmlHead method

This method is used to create the header section of the html
report. As you can see in the below figure, we have the html
header of the report. The method simply writes the html code in
the report file.

No	Test_Id	Test_Case_Name		Test_Description

Figure 7 - Header Section of the Report

3. createTestCaseLog Method

This method is used to apppend the log of each test case. The
method writes the action performed by selenium webdriver into
variable gtestcaselog. It takes 2 parameters. First parameter
specifies the pass/fail status of the step while second parameter
specifies the data to append to the gtestcaselog variable.

```
String strhtml="";
if (intStatus == 1)
strhtml = "<span style='color:green'> Pass : </span>
" ;
else if (intStatus == 2)
strhtml = "<span style='color:red'> Fail   :
</span> ";
else if (intStatus == 3)
strhtml = "<span style='color:maroon'> Warning :
</span> ";
else if (intStatus == 4)
strhtml = "<span> Info   : </span> " ;
```

```
gtestcaselog.append(strhtml).append(str).append("<br
/>");
```

Figure 8 - testlog

4. createTestReport Method

This method is used to create the report for the current test case. It writes all details of the current test case like No, Test_Id, Test_Case_Name, Test_Description and Status to the report file.

Figure 9 – TestReport

5. getTimeDiff Method

This method is used to find the time difference between 2 time stamps.

```
float diff = t2 - t1;

if (interval.equalsIgnoreCase("min"))
      diff = diff / (1000*60);
else
      diff = diff / 1000;

DecimalFormat df=new DecimalFormat("0.00");
String formate = df.format(diff);
```

5. readCell Method

This method is used to read the cell value in the excel sheet. It takes 2 parameters – row and column number.

```
if  (rowObj.getCell(colNum).getCellType() == 1)
```

```
    x =
rowObj.getCell(colNum).getStringCellValue();
else if  (rowObj.getCell(colNum).getCellType() == 0)
x = "" +
(int)rowObj.getCell(colNum).getNumericCellValue();
```

6. writeCell Method

This method is used to write the cell value in the excel sheet. It takes 3 parameters – row and column number and value to write to.

```
rowObj.getCell(colNum).setCellValue((String) data);
```

3.5 Function Library (Keyword Library)

Keyword_Library class provides methods that are mapped to the keywords in test data sheet.

There are 2 kinds of keywords.
1. Functionality specific keyword (E.g. Login)
2. Generic Keyword

Some of the most important Generic Keywords are mentioned below.
1. xls_Enter_Data
2. xls_Verify_Data
3. xls_Is_Displayed

Let us have a look at each of them.

1. xls_Enter_Data Method

This method is used to enter the data in the application based upon web control type such as editbox, combobox, checkbox, Buttons and links etc.

We can enter the data in multiple controls using this method. The input to this method is object information. It will split the object information in array and then try to perform operation on each object based upon its type.

```
String []ct = controlType.split(";");
String []cn = controlName.split(";");
String []cv = controlValues.split(";");
```

First it checks whether the given object exists in the webpage using getElement method.

```
e = getElement(method,cname);

if (e==null)
{
Futil.createTestCaseLog("Web Element " +
curControlType + " -> "+ curControlName + " not
found", 2);
        return false;

}
else{

Futil.createTestCaseLog("Web Element " +
curControlType + " -> "+ curControlName + " found",
1);

}
```

If element is not found on the webpage, it will return false. Otherwise it will switch to one of the cases mentioned in below code. For example if the element is a link, it will jump to link case and click on the given link.

```java
switch (ct[i].toLowerCase().trim())

{
    case "weblist":
    Select select=new Select(e);
    Futil.createTestCaseLog("Value selected " +
curControlValue  ,4);

select.selectByVisibleText(curControlValue);
            break;

    case "webedit":
Futil.createTestCaseLog("Value entered is -> <b> " +
curControlValue + "</b>"  ,4);
        e.sendKeys(curControlValue);
        break;
    case "webbutton":
    e.click();
    break;

    case "link":

((JavascriptExecutor)
TestExecutor.wb).executeScript("arguments[0].click()
",e);
        Thread.sleep(5000);

            break;

}
```

2. xls_Verify_Data Method

This method is used to verify the data in the application based upon web control type such as editbox, combobox, checkbox etc.

We can verify the data in multiple controls using this method. The input to this method is object information. It will split the object information in array and then try to verify the object based upon its type.

```
String []ct = controlType.split(";");
String []cn = controlName.split(";");
String []cv = controlValues.split(";");
```

First it checks whether the given object exists in the webpage using getElement method.

```
e = getElement(method,cname);

if (e==null)
{
Futil.createTestCaseLog("Web Element " +
curControlType + " -> "+ curControlName + " not
found", 2);
        return false;

}
else{

Futil.createTestCaseLog("Web Element " +
curControlType + " -> "+ curControlName + " found",
1);

}
```

If element is not found on the webpage, it will return false. Otherwise it will switch to one of the cases mentioned in below code. For example if the element is a link, it will jump to link case and click on the given link.

```
switch (ct[i].toLowerCase().trim())

{
    case "weblist":
Select comboBox = new Select(e);
actualValue =
comboBox.getFirstSelectedOption().getAttribute("valu
e");
            break;
    case "webedit":

    actualValue = e.getAttribute("value");
            break;
}
```

3. xls_Is_Displayed Method
This method is used to check if web controls like editbox, combobox, checkbox are displayed on the webpage.

4. getElement Method
This method is used to find the web Elements (controls) like editbox, combobox, checkbox on the webpage. This method takes 2 parameters method and name.
For example – if the method is id and name is fname, it will try to find the element on the web page having id = fname.
If element is found on the web page, it will be returned back to calling method. Otherwise it will return null value.

```
if (method.trim().equalsIgnoreCase("id"))
e = TestExecutor.wb.findElement(By.id(cname));
else if (method.trim().equalsIgnoreCase("class"))
```

```java
e =
TestExecutor.wb.findElement(By.className(cname));
else if (method.trim().equalsIgnoreCase("label"))
{
        List <WebElement> we =
TestExecutor.wb.findElements(By.tagName("label"));

for(int i=0;i<we.size();i++)
         if
(we.get(i).getText().equalsIgnoreCase(cname))
              id = we.get(i).getAttribute("for");
     e = TestExecutor.wb.findElement(By.id(id));

}
else if  (method.equalsIgnoreCase("name"))
e = TestExecutor.wb.findElement(By.name(cname));
else if  (method.equalsIgnoreCase("xpath"))
{

     if (cname.startsWith("href*"))
//Dangling metacharacter error will occur if cname
contains special regular expression character'
//to escape special characters you must escape it
using \\
{
     String href =  cname.split("\\*")[1];
Futil.createTestCaseLog("finding link with href " +
href, 4);
e =
TestExecutor.wb.findElement(By.xpath("//a[contains(@
href,'" + href + "')]"));


              }
     else
              e =
TestExecutor.wb.findElement(By.xpath(cname));
}
else if  (method.equalsIgnoreCase("linktext"))
e = TestExecutor.wb.findElement(By.linkText(cname));
```

4. Hybrid Automation framework

In this chapter, you will learn about how to design hybrdi automation frameworks in Selenium Webdriver.

Hybrid framework is the combination of data driven and keyword driven frameworks.

The Hybrid-Driven Testing pattern is made up of a number of reusable modules / function libraries that are developed with the following characteristics in mind:

- Maintainability – significantly reduces the test maintenance effort
- Reusability – due to modularity of test cases and library functions
- Reliability – due to advanced error handling and scenario recovery
- Measurability – customisable reporting of test results ensure quality